The Box

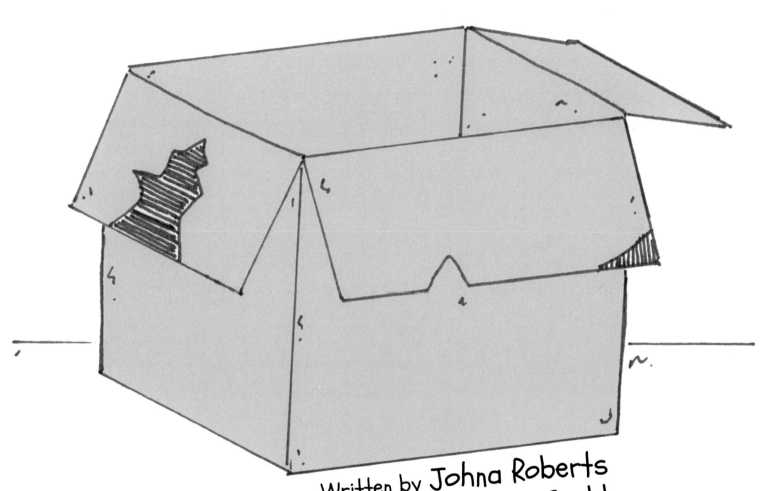

Written by Johna Roberts
Illustrated by Amber Crabb

WestBow Press books may be ordered through booksellers or by contacting:

WestBow Press
A Division of Thomas Nelson & Zondervan
1663 Liberty Drive
Bloomington, IN 47403
www.westbowpress.com
844-714-3454

ISBN: 979-8-3850-2981-5 (sc)
ISBN: 979-8-3850-2982-2 (hc)
ISBN: 979-8-3850-2983-9 (e)

Library of Congress Control Number: 2024914888

Print information available on the last page.

WestBow Press rev. date: 10/28/2024

WESTBOW
PRESS®
A DIVISION OF THOMAS NELSON
& ZONDERVAN

The Box

I have a box that fits me,
The perfect shape and height.
And in this box I find me, smug
And smart and always right.

2

So I display this box here
And proudly call it mine.
I ask my friend to sit inside
My box so fair and fine!

But when she tries to fit there,
   Oh, no! She just won't go!
Her leg pops out, she pulls it in,
   Then out pops her elbow!

Her head, it bends the corner;
A new dent for her toe!
I try so hard to make her fit,
But no, she just won't go!

I search and find another
Good friend to fit my mold.
I catch my breath—he just might fit
If he can hold that fold!

But then I see a finger—
It's poking through a crack.
I push it in, but then I spy
A split across his back!

Now I'm getting angrier!
It's shaped so perfectly.
This box should fit just anyone,
You see—it's right for me!

I get a little frantic
With everyone I meet;

I try to cram them in my box,

Their heads down to their feet!

I'm so mad, I throw a fit.
I rage and stomp and cry!
What's wrong with all these people here?
Why can't they fit inside?

Then, breaking through my rampage,
A friend so kind and calm
Says, "Settle down and take a breath;
You're viewing this all wrong.

"See, God made your box to be
The perfect fit for you;
But hers and his and all of theirs
Fit them precisely too.

"God never asks His children
To squeeze where they can't fit;

Each box is custom-crafted for
The treasure kept in it.

"He made them all—the boxes—
And everyone within.
Yes, He's aware that every box
Is beaten up by sin.

"God knows that sin has broken
The hearts and souls therein.
So, friend, come near and look from here.
Let's start this all again."

Then in my mind I see those
I'd thrown a fit about,
Becoming like a masterpiece
From inside to without.

God's still, small voice calls each one
To take the nail-marked hand;
And those who come,
He leads them to
A higher place to stand.

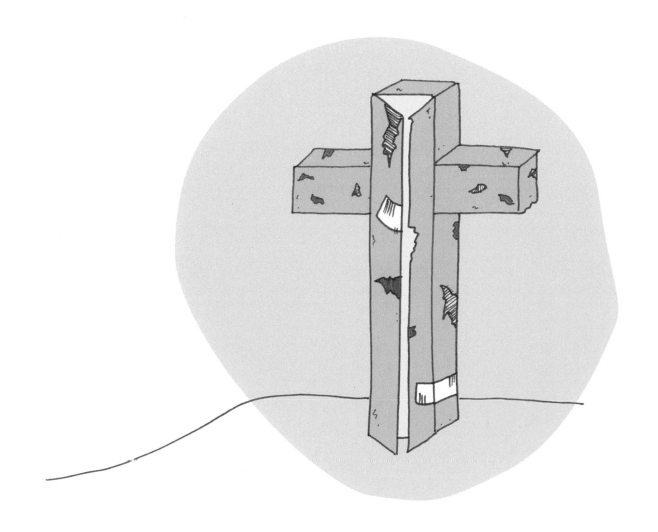

In that place I see a Box—
It's shaped so differently.
It's here that Christ defeated sin-
Eternal victory!

East to west, the sides stretch wide
To reach the farthest soul;
And from the earth it towers high
To mend the gaping hole.

It spans the gap of sin from
The perfect, holy God
To all who come to Him by faith
In Jesus's sinless blood.

At this Box, all those who come
Ashamed and starved of worth,
Repentant, then transformed by grace,
Receive new life—rebirth!

Each boxy frame is still the same
 God-designed creation;
But inside-out they shine the light
 Of joy in true salvation.

Then, dismayed, I see myself,
All proud and knowing best;
Here in the shadow of this Box
I'm just like all the rest.

When I see my sinful heart,
My only hope is grace.
I turn and run repentantly
Up to that holy place.

God, my gracious Maker, draws
This selfish, prideful me
Up to His Box; by faith I stand,
Forgiven, new, and free!

I'm the same as when I came,
As far as outwardly;
But inside I'm reborn to grow
In Christ, who died for me.

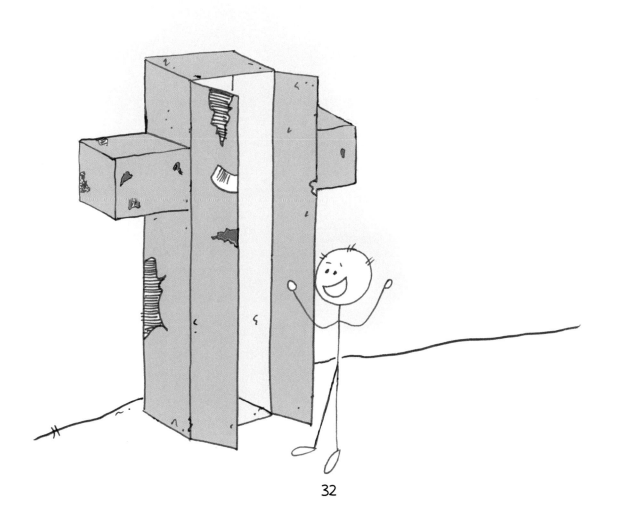

I'm not like any other, and
No one is just like me.

The shape of each is beautiful—
Those freed, and those who seek.

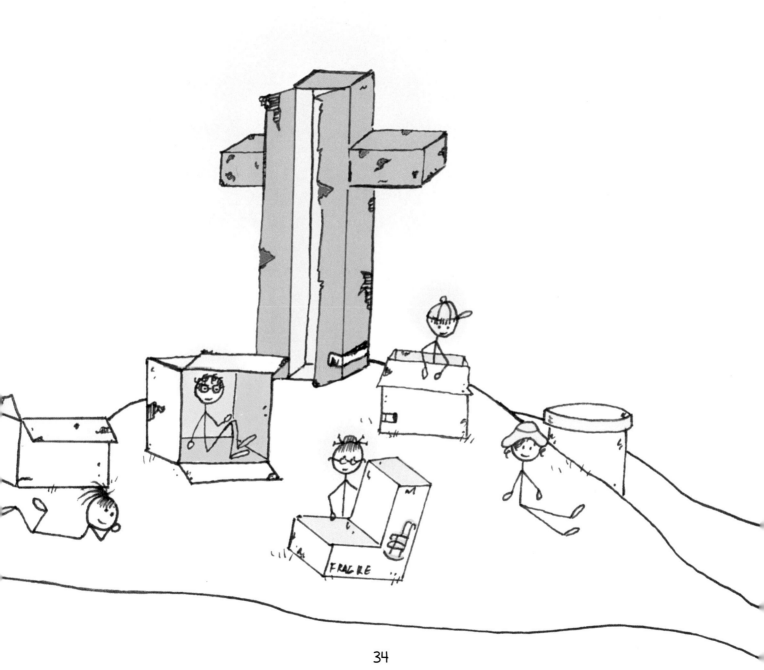

I won't expect another
To fit my box today;
We all need Jesus just the same—
His Box—The only Way!

I have a box that fits me,
The perfect shape and height;
From here, I love each treasured soul
And God, with all my might!

Genesis 1:27 (ESV)

"So God created man in his own image, in the image of God he created him; male and female he created them."

Psalm 139:13-14 (ESV)

"For you formed my inward parts; you knitted me together in my mother's womb. I praise you, for I am fearfully and wonderfully made. Wonderful are your works; my soul knows it well."

Romans 3:23-25a (ESV)

"For all have sinned and fall short of the glory of God, and are justified by his grace as a gift, through the redemption that is in Christ Jesus, whom God put forward as a propitiation by his blood, to be received by faith."

John 14:6 (ESV)

"Jesus said to him, 'I am the way, and the truth, and the life.
No one comes to the Father except through me.'"

Romans 10:4–13 (ESV)

"If you confess with your mouth that Jesus is Lord and believe in your heart that God raised him from the dead, you will be saved. For with the heart one believes and is justified, and with the mouth one confesses and is saved. For the Scripture says, 'Everyone who believes in him will not be put to shame.' There is no distinction between Jew and Greek; for the same Lord is Lord of all, bestowing his riches on all who call on him. For 'everyone who calls on the name of the Lord will be saved.'"

Psalm 34:5 (ESV)

"Those who look to him are radiant, and their faces shall never be ashamed."

About the Author

Johna Roberts has written poems and songs for most of her life, but The Box is her first book publication. She is a music teacher with over 35 years' experience in piano, early childhood music, children's choirs, and elementary general music. She loves the way God uses music, lyrics, and stories to unify and draw people to His Kingdom. Johna's husband, Chris, is also a musician, and they serve at EastPoint Baptist Church in Midwest City, Oklahoma, where she teaches Sunday School and Chris is the lead pastor. They have six children who also love and serve God with their unique gifts. Johna's hobbies include writing, playing the piano, sewing, embroidering, and cooking meals to bring her family together.

About the Illustrator

Amber Crabb has blessed countless people over the years with her artwork, but The Box is her first time to be published. She is a first grade teacher at Christian Heritage Academy in Del City, Oklahoma, where she also leads in teacher mentoring and curriculum development. She and her husband, Jimmy, are leaders at EastPoint Baptist Church in Midwest City, Oklahoma, where Amber teaches Sunday School and Jimmy is an associate pastor. Both are eager to serve and have taken mission trips all over the world, sharing the love of Jesus wherever He leads them to an open door.

About the Image Editor

Jill Wells has the heart of a teacher, the skill of an artist, and a steadfast commitment to her mission of redeeming the fine arts for the glory of God. She is the high school art teacher and art education mentor at Christian Heritage Academy in Del City, Oklahoma. She, her husband Josh, and their four children are active members of Village Baptist Church in Oklahoma City, and they lead a Bible study group in their home. Jill enjoys coaching soccer and other sports, loves outdoor activities, and creates her own artwork whenever she has opportunity.

Printed in the United States
by Baker & Taylor Publisher Services